THE JOURNEY
OF
THE SUN

THE JOURNEY
OF
THE SUN

✳

ANA MOYANO and ADRIANA URIBE

iUniverse, Inc.
New York   Bloomington

The Journey of the Sun

iUniverse books may be ordered through booksellers or by contacting:

iUniverse
1663 Liberty Drive
Bloomington, IN 47403
www.iuniverse.com
1-800-Authors (1-800-288-4677)

ISBN: 978-0-595-52024-4 (pbk)
ISBN: 978-0-595-62116-3 (ebk)

Printed in the United States of America

iUniverse Rev. Date 12/18/2008

TABLE OF CONTENTS

INTRODUCTION

WE ARE SMALL GRAINS OF SAND IN THE OCEAN THAT IS THE UNIVERSE. THIS IS A DIFFICULT TRUTH TO remember. Realizing we are part of the universe gives us the possibility to learn the lessons we have not understood or completed in the past. At that moment, we stop wondering "why is this happening to me" and become brave and excited as we disentangle the mystery of the real self. The path to follow opens clearly and the events we face become exciting opportunities to find personal clues to our own existence.

Astrology is a very useful instrument to interpret the lessons the universe is teaching us. By observing our solar system and understanding how its energy relates to our personal experiences, we open up to the wisdom nature stores. Every civilization looked into the skies searching for answers and found them through conscious observation and study. Observation and study is all that is required to achieve a deeper connection with your inner self and accept life as part of an evolving learning cycle.

We created this book as a first step to help you understand your connection with the universe. Use it as a tool to explore your birth energy and experience change as the sun travels through the zodiac. Astrology has related the solar system and constellations to our earthly lives and through this process has defined influences and potentials which you will learn about in this book. This learning will take place to the extent you accept to use your experiences in life as part of your learning process and not merely see them as isolated events beyond your control.

When used properly, a tool has the potential to help you create, fix, build, destroy, modify, adjust or transform your surroundings. Tools can become indispensable to have your work done, but this is not the case. Although human kind needs only serious commitment to work consciously in order to evolve, astrology as a tool can make the process clearer. The purpose of this book is to introduce you to astrology, help you to look inside yourself and find answers about your own experiences.

Once you develop the capability to observe yourself and relate your experiences to external circumstances and the lessons you can learn from them, every day becomes an exciting adventure where your ordinary life holds priceless possibilities for inner growth and evolution. At that point, astrology will be your companion and you will be taking full advantage of the training you have acquired through the practices and explanations written in this book.

PREPARE FOR THE JOURNEY

The Journey of the Sun

HOW TO USE THIS BOOK

The Journey of the Sun does not hold complex theories or analysis of the universe. This book has been made to give you the opportunity to find your center and work from there with your own vision and intuition, while connecting with the universe through the ancient wisdom of astrology. With the help of astrology you will be empowered to understand and experience growth as a human being.

As this is going to be a practical experience, we advise you to follow the steps and recommendations in this chapter before starting to explore the birth signs. A little preparation now will make a big difference in the quality of your experience in the long run.

- Read the following pages carefully as they summarize the procedure you will follow on each birth sign. The steps explain how meditation, observation and analysis work and evolve from an individual perspective.

- *The Journey of the Sun* and *The Journal of the Journey* work together. This way, you use the wisdom of astrology on your own experiences. Your potential in life is limitless and to use astrology to maximize it will provide you with exciting experiences worth recording and keeping close to you. Use the Journal of the Journey with this purpose in mind and along the guidelines of the Journey of the Sun.

- If you would like to know more about astrology, read the chapter dedicated to reference (A Brief Look into Astrology) and seek out additional information in other publications. This might help you feel more comfortable about the experience and practices you will develop with this book.

- Follow the sequence and methods we have set. As with everything in nature, there is a time for each phase. You cannot harvest when you have neither planted the seed nor nurtured the growing tree.

- Start your astrological experience by choosing the birth sign from the date you start reading this book. The Journey of the Sun has been organized according to the movement of the sun throughout the twelve birth signs or constellations that form the zodiac and all birth signs, observed carefully and consciously, can give you the clues and answers you need at a particular moment in time.

- As you develop the working method for each birth sign you will witness events that you normally tend to think of as coincidences. Casual encounters with people you have not seen in a while, dreams, unexpected events and personally meaningful situations can represent clues about your path. Be attentive to these events and do not disregard them as unrelated. By exploring them and possibly recording them in the Journal of the Journey, you will keep an attitude of observation and exploration that will refine and provide priceless clues along this journey.

STEP ONE: OBSERVATION OF THE UNIVERSE

MEDITATION AND VISUALIZATION

Regardless of how small we seem to be compared with the cosmos, we are influenced and influence the universe continuously. A constant process of exchange exists in our universe and we are an active part of it. Meditation and visualization are techniques that facilitate our awareness of this interaction. Our connection with the universe becomes stronger and clearer as we practice meditation on a regular basis.

Observing our universe can be done by focusing our attention either externally or internally. Science, technology and a deeper understanding of the world we inhabit, is the result of careful observation of the external environment. Likewise, philosophy and spirituality achieve knowledge by looking inwardly.

Some of the greatest pioneers of science and philosophy are often described as quiet and sharp-eyed children who reached deep understanding of their subject of observation. Likewise, you will be observing your personal universe. In the process, you will gain knowledge which will allow you to make exciting discoveries and use them for your personal growth.

Meditation as a practice gives you the chance to be aware while in a state of inner peace and relaxation. It is not difficult and does not require more than determination to take the time to do it. It may seem difficult in the beginning as the mind wants to wander incessantly and creates the very same thoughts we want to avoid. The easiest way to master meditation is relaxing and letting go of any thought the mind tries to impose. Instead of actively rejecting these thoughts, acknowledge them and release them indifferently. As you meditate more often these thoughts will become silent and eventually will vanish. You will find yourself in a state of tranquility you initially thought impossible.

Visualizing is a part of the meditation exercise where you direct your mind gently towards set images, in order to open doorways to relaxation and communication with deeper stages of awareness. Visualizing or imagining is a good way to remove intrusive thoughts your mind is accustomed to create and to focus instead on the here-and-now. This is the point at which all practical, positive change occurs and to be in this state gives you an enormous amount of power over your own life. The way you meditate will be unique and personal. It will vary depending mainly on what you have to observe about yourself.

MEDITATION EXERCISE

The following meditation exercise facilitates a cleansing process which is not only relevant to this book but to live a fuller life. Meditation has been proven to improve general health conditions, provide release for tension and improve concentration. It is a technique of mental self control which provides a space to detach yourself from stressful situations and harmful feelings.

This exercise is set to last fifteen minutes or less; a very short period of time if you think of the potential benefits in the long term. Likewise, we recommend that you read these pages thoroughly and make sure you understand the exercise in itself before setting out to do it. Take the time to familiarize yourself with the steps to follow. These have a very logical sequence to make you aware of your body starting from your feet and continuing towards your head. You just need to make sure you give enough attention to each part of your body during the relaxation process.

It is normal to have physical experiences and many of our clients had to struggle to stay awake the first few times they meditated because their bodies needed to reenergize. However, with practice they learned to relax and preferred to extend the time of the exercise as it proved to have a positive general effect for the rest of the day.

START YOUR MEDITATION EXERCISE

Choose a place where you know you will not be disturbed during the session, which should take approximately fifteen minutes. If your time is limited, make sure to set an alarm clock so that you don't interrupt your exercise to check the time. Distractions caused by outside noise can be eliminated playing soft instrumental music at low volume.

Once you have set the place, choose the birth sign you want to work with and read the phrase in the beginning of the chapter of the Journey of the Sun. Do not read further in the chapter at this stage. You only need to remember this phrase during meditation.

To start the meditation, find a comfortable position sitting on a normal chair, with your spine straight and feet resting on the ground. Your hands should rest on your legs or knees. You should feel comfortable in this position.

Start by breathing slowly and effortlessly. Concentrate on breathing while your body becomes acquainted with the position you have adopted and your mind calms down. Start breathing gently from the base of your lungs once you feel ready. Imagine a balloon in your stomach inflating as you inhale slowly and make an effort to store air in the base of your lungs by expanding your abdomen. As the imaginary balloon fills with air, start expanding your lungs and visualizing it expanding until your lungs are filled with their maximum capacity without causing any stress or tension. Once you have reached this point, hold your breath for three seconds and start to exhale slowly and gently imagining the balloon going back to its original position as the air leaves your lungs.

Practice this technique a few times. Once you feel comfortable with this conscious breathing, focus your attention on your feet and ankles as you inhale. Visualize your feet, toes, toenails, soles and ankles while you inhale. Keep concentrating on your feet as you hold your breath and exhale, feeling all the tension and discomfort which has accumulated in your feet being removed as the air goes out of your body.

Continue the breathing exercise becoming aware of each part of your body and traveling upwards with your attention. Feel your calves, legs and knees and follow the same procedure. Always remember your breathing and allow your body to release any tension accumulated in your muscles, bones, tendons or skin, as you exhale. Our bodies keep perfect memories of all circumstances surrounding us and therefore they will need cleansing as much as our minds.

After you have cleansed legs and feet, move your attention towards your hips, the base of your spine, genitalia and internal organs. All internal organs in your body will connect and cleanse with this rhythmic breathing as you continue this exercise. You will feel progressively calmed and relaxed, internally and externally.

Visualize each part of your body in an ascending order while inhaling and exhaling to release tension. Continue the breathing exercise relaxing your abdomen and the base of your spine and upwards toward your chest, lungs and breasts. Focus on your shoulders, arms, elbows, hands, fingers and fingernails. Always check if you find points of particular tension or discomfort and, if necessary, repeat the breathing exercise more than once if you feel there is more tension to be expelled from a particular area.

Powerful feelings and corporeal sensations may appear while you are meditating. Nausea, overwhelming sadness and a need to cry, are common examples. Do not feel disturbed by these. Interrupt the meditation and allow yourself these experiences as they are related to its cleansing effect. Our bodies hold a perfect record of all that disturbs us and what we fail to recognize consciously. When we meditate the body takes the opportunity to release negative energy that could otherwise become harmful. You can continue with your breathing exercises and meditation once you feel better.

When you reach your shoulders and back, be aware of keeping your spine straight so that while you progress on this breathing exercise, all tension is released when you exhale.

The last part of the breathing exercise is focusing on the head and face. As you inhale check your facial muscles and scalp so that these can relax as well. Once you have done this breathing exercise examining every part of your body, continue breathing gently and normally. If you find any point of tension you forgot to eliminate, use the breathing exercise again as many times as you need to complete your relaxation.

While you are relaxed and breathing gently, remember the phrase you read before starting the meditation. If exact words do not come to you, the meaning of the phrase, the personal meaning it has for you, will do. Build your own phrase if you cannot remember the original one and repeat it continuously. You should repeat it until you feel you will not forget it and it is safely implanted in your mind for the rest of the day and days to come. This repetition should not be automatic but rather conscious, absorbing the meaning of the words and how they resonate with your personal experience.

The techniques explained in this book are simple but effective and require no previous experience. Your results will be proportionate to your involvement but do not judge them against any set expectations. The whole experience is unique and individual. As you progress through the birth signs and spend time on the exercises described in this book you will start noticing additional messages that concern your own life and journey. These messages might come to you as intrusive thoughts during the meditation. Acknowledge them and continue your visualization or breathing. Gradually you will start recognizing as matter of fact that you have access to a state of inner peace which opens your connection with the universe.

STEP TWO: OBSERVATION OF THE INNER SELF

GATHERING YOUR EXPERIENCES

To observe the inner self means to be aware of your own actions, feelings and thoughts. Very often we behave like machines with a set of predictable responses and forget we have the capability to choose our reactions and understand our feelings in depth. Remembering constantly that we must observe our inner self means that we are willing to take a step forward towards our personal evolution and growth regardless of how difficult it may seem at times.

The last section of the book is called the Journal of the Journey. It is a mini-diary or scrapbook to store and collect personal information you feel or know that can be meaningful. Either by writing it down or by keeping material pieces (photographs, candy wrappers, newspaper cuttings, etc) you can easily relate to your experiences or memories, thus developing a conscious research that will prove rewarding as you advance in the exercises for each birth sign.

If you do not seem to find any connection, the Journal of the Journey will give you some general hints to help you identify feelings and emotions related with each zodiacal sign.

During the meditation exercise, thoughts, memories and ideas will interrupt you. Any particular event that draws your attention should be written down in your Journal of the Journey after finishing the exercise. This does not mean you need to cling to those thoughts while the meditation takes place. When the session is over, you will be able to remember the most significant ones and these are the ones that should be recorded. Be attentive in your daily life and do not overlook your dreams, ideas or thoughts.

It will be useful to take into account the questions enclosed in the Journal of the Journey to work with each birth sign as well. What you record might contain important keys to resolving questions that come into your mind while experiencing each sign. Your inner observation has always been your greatest self-help instrument and it can open the door to knowledge and wisdom to understand your own experiences in life.

STEP THREE: CONNECTING HEART AND MIND

- READING AND UNDERSTANDING -

Throughout the Journey of the Sun, you will constantly be observing and gathering experiences. You can acquire a more structured explanation of the birth sign you decide to study by reading the corresponding chapter in this book. Read each chapter as if it was a recipe you are preparing and remember that time is required for a meal to be ready to taste. You will have to be attentive and check constantly to avoid spoiling the flavor.

There are weekly exercises as you go through each birth sign. These will prompt answers to your questions and doubts. In this way you will also experience the evolution of the birth sign as you observe how you relate to the outside world. Your notes can be complemented during this step as you are also recording your feelings and thoughts while the exercises in question take place.

When you read the corresponding chapter of the book, concentrate on the information and explanation of the birth sign you chose, applying it to your current situation in life. There is a learning message in every chapter. The characteristics of each sign have also been written for general information and you might find that some of them are particularly relevant in your present circumstances. They explain the way the sun expresses its energy through the birth sign in question.

A BRIEF LOOK INTO ASTROLOGY

How astrology looks at the Universe

As humans we might have first related changes in nature with the existence of continuous movement in the skies. Only after extensive study and observation, we were able to establish that there was a perfect and complex exchange in nature in our planet but also as part of the solar system. At that time, we must have acquired the capabilities to determine and forecast the seasons, the times for sowing and harvest, the change of tides: eventually we were able to establish temporal cycles and organize human activity accordingly.

Wise men and women have studied the movement of the stars. This deep and constant study has given us the opportunity to understand how the universe works and the way it relates to our own experience in this planet.

Astronomy continues studying the universe and establishing mathematical records that lead to constant new advances in our knowledge of the universe even beyond the solar system. Astrology, on the other hand, continues studying the universe from a different approach: in relation to our planet and the human experience. Humans, nature and the universe are subtly interconnected. Throughout history, astrologers found answers to human existence which made astrology grow and become a generous source of knowledge and analysis to understand personal, cultural and generational experiences.

Birth charts

By establishing the position of the planets, stars and constellations at the moment of birth, you acquire a map of the sky (seen from earth) that is called a birth chart or natal chart. Professional astrologers calculate these according to your exact date, time and place of birth to determine how these elements are located and can influence your personality, potentials, behavior and even events you might be prone to experience in your lifetime. A birth chart can be calculated for anything that has a commencement date, for instance, the beginning of a business enterprise, as a forecast for the year ahead, etc.

However, the most important information from a birth chart is the way the energy from different planets and constellations can manifest itself in your life and what is the best way to take advantage of it. In this book you will explore how the energy represented by the sun influences every area of your life. This requires you to understand that you possess the natural ability to connect with the universe and become aware that events you experience in your life have a purpose and belong in a bigger, perfect plan.

Points of observation

Heliocentric view refers to our perception of the solar system when our point of observation is the sun. Imagine you were sitting in the sun: you would observe all the planets of the solar system rotating around you. In astrology, however, we use the **geocentric view**, since our point of observation is the earth. In the past, people pictured the stars -including the sun- and planets rotating around the earth. The center of observation could be any planet or star, but in the case of astrology it will be the earth, since it is the planet we inhabit. The geocentric view helped to define seasons, orientation and cycles in nature.

The geocentric view also gives us the chance to locate the sun in the constellations surrounding the earth, and to determine when the sun passes through each of them during the year. If you can picture yourself staring at the skies, think of the sun as a funnel that absorbs energy as it describes an imaginary circle around the earth. The circle has twelve sections which would be the constellations or zodiacal signs. Our planet receives energy from the sun and its energy will manifest in a particular way depending on the constellation it is crossing at a certain point in time. The constellations correspond to the twelve birth signs.

The same image of the funnel is applicable to other planets and celestial bodies in the universe. They work as funnels delivering energy from the constellations in a distinctive way. This is how astrology came to relate events between planetary movement and human life. Astrology holds knowledge that was not reached accidentally and cannot be considered superstition. It has taken the age of humanity to understand our connection with the universe and, as such, it should be honored and used as a tool for further evolution.

The birth signs

The sun seen from our planet passes through twelve constellations during the year. These constellations are represented by the birth signs each of us belong to according to our date of birth. For instance, using a geocentric view, on February 6th it was in the constellation of the water bearer which corresponds to the sign of Aquarius. Therefore, if you were born on that day, your birth sign would be Aquarius. In astrology, the position where the sun appears to be on the day you were born represents a learning process we will develop throughout our lives. A person from Aquarius will learn during his lifetime the characteristics and qualities needed to be an Aquarian. Every sign has the potential to show us the highest levels of evolution. It is our task to unlock the lessons that the birth signs provide and to develop that potential to reach the best expression of their energy.

If you are not certain of which is your birth sign, as you might have been born on a day when the sun moves from one constellation (or birth sign) to the next, it is recommended to have your birth chart calculated by a professional astrologer. The astrologer will take your exact date, time and place of birth to determine your birth sign and avoid any confusion. For instance, if you were born on November 23rd, it may not be clear whether your birth sign is Scorpio or Sagittarius.

To know your birth sign is important, as the sun carries different types of energy that manifests itself throughout your life. The sun is like a funnel transporting the energy of a constellation into our planet. In the case of the birth sign, it means we are born with the energy of this constellation as it is illuminated by the sun and we will feel it acting distinctively throughout our lives. Just as we can read a book better by directing light to its pages, the characteristics of a birth sign become more evident when the sun is in that particular constellation at the time of birth.

Our birth sign could be understood as a body of traits that will show up in diverse circumstances of our life, giving us certain potential to develop as we define our identity. When you see a birth chart graphic, either calculated by an astrologer or computer generated, you realize each constellation was in a particular position at the moment of your birth. As rotation takes place during the year, the sun will pass through the twelve zodiacal signs and will accentuate the energy of each constellation, allowing it to be manifest in your life. Therefore, it is important to understand the sequence of the sun's rotation as well in order to relate personal experiences throughout the year and throughout life.

Classification of birth signs

The twelve birth signs have been grouped according to common characteristics:

BIRTH SIGNS DIVIDED BY ELEMENT

There are four elements that give their characteristics to the birth signs: fire, water, air and earth. These characteristics cannot be seen as physical, but rather as pictorial ideas that relate to the nature of these birth signs and how they would become apparent in facts and behaviors from people who belong to these signs.

Fire: Aries, Leo and Sagittarius belong to this element. They are characterized by radiant and direct energy that can also be perceived when we think about fire. Like the spark that creates fire, these birth signs have the quality to bring intuition and energy.

Water: Birth signs belonging to the water element are characterized by the emotional energy they possess. The water can be soft and subtle, as we see it when the ocean is calm, or strong and powerful when waves crash. This is easy to relate to our emotions, sometimes calm; energetic in other instances. Cancer, Scorpio and Pisces belong to the water element.

Air: The energy in air birth signs is associated with breathing, communication and the world of thoughts and ideas. The wind transports the seeds in the land to preserve life, and our breathing and communication allow us to create and maintain constant interaction with our environment, nurturing and giving us the chance to express our thoughts. The air element gives these attributes to Aquarius, Libra and Gemini.

Earth: The energy of the earth element can be understood by its relationship with our physical senses. When we plant a seed, we know the result of this will be something as concrete and material as a plant. Its fruits will also have the same physical nature. Our planet has a material and concrete quality which we perceive through our senses, and birth signs belonging to the earth element are characterized by the real nature they require to manifest. These birth signs are Taurus, Virgo and Capricorn.

BIRTH SIGNS DIVIDED BY POLARITY

We perceive our environment through polarity. From the beginning of time, people understood that there is always a positive and negative quality in everything. Black and white, feminine and masculine, right and left, light and dark, positive and negative, are a few examples of polarity. These do not imply one extreme is better than the other. Instead, one cannot be considered possible without its opposite, since balance exists only when both are present.

This polarity exists also in birth signs. The masculine quality belongs to birth signs of fire and air as their creative nature is expressed in these elements. Earth and water elements have the quality of receptivity, which relates to the feminine nature.

◊   *A note about Axis: the birth chart is normally drawn as a circle with twelve divisions, each one corresponding to a birth sign. As a result, each sign would have an opposite to form an axis. Both signs forming an axis are opposite and complementary. As any other polarity, one cannot exist without the other. Each birth sign would have its opposite and usually the exercises suggested in this book examine both sides of a given situation. There are always two sides to consider to every manifestation and it is important to keep this in mind because opposites complete each other and the key is to integrate them rather than favor or reject one of them.*

BIRTH SIGNS DIVIDED BY MODE

Birth, growth and transformation are seen continuously in nature. We will see the same process related to the energy the sun gives us as it passes through the birth signs. The energy from each element in nature is manifested distinctively and with different intensity. This is also the case with birth signs. For example, if we think of fire and relate it with the birth signs classified under the fire element (Aries, Leo and Sagittarius) each birth will express the fire energy in a distinctive way according with the process of birth, growth and transformation.

Birth: Cardinal birth signs (Aries, Cancer, Libra and Capricorn) represent the birth of a process. These will be signs related with a starting drive. Taking again the example of the fire element, the cardinal birth sign which is Aries would correspond to a strong impulse, like a first spark when we light a match.

Growth: Fixed birth signs (Leo, Scorpio, Aquarius and Taurus) are those which maintain and stabilize initial intensity. Here, the initial drive becomes a stable and controlled flow of energy. The first spark that lighted the match becomes a flame.

Transformation: Finally, mutable birth signs (Sagittarius, Pisces, Gemini and Virgo) transform the energy. The flow of energy maintained by fixed birth signs evolves and transcends its original nature. The flame has burned the match and, although extinct, it has turned it into ashes.

In the following pages you will find a section for each birth sign. In the first page of every section you will find a sentence which you should remember during your meditation exercise. You will also find the characteristics of the birth sign according to the classification explained above.

Although this is just for reference, it might help you to identify better the characteristics of each birth sign and to be more attentive to the energy the sun is likely to manifest during its transit through each birth sign.

So now, let's begin.

The Journey of the Sun

BIRTH SIGNS

This is me.

ARIES

21ˢᵗ March – 19ᵗʰ April

Aries: Fire, masculine, cardinal.

It would be easier to feel Aries energy than to talk about it. It is like trying to define with words what you felt when you were born. Aries is the initial birth sign. This is related with the beginning of spring in the northern hemisphere; the beginning of life. Once we are born our first breath represents the moment when we are defined by ourselves. Our limit is not our mother's womb anymore, but our own body which starts its own breathing cycle and defines its own identity, unique and special.

Imagine Aries like a new room, where we have just the walls, door and a window, but everything else still has to be done. We know it will need colors, decoration, curtains, fixtures, furniture and so on before we can define whether it will be a bedroom or an office. The new room we are facing holds all the potential to be developed into something particular and unique. Aries is that initial force which needs definition.

Aries is that great beginning force in us that has not yet been educated and needs to be recognized. It can be explosive and unexpected and has all the energy and impulsiveness of a child. This is what Aries will represent in our lives every time we arrive into a new stage or when we start something new. In Aries there is a lot to work on in order to define ourselves for what we are and what we have achieved.

Regardless of our age and wisdom, there are always new beginnings. The way we face a new start should be spontaneous and natural. Beginnings are always full of accidental events that might produce frustration in us. But this is the moment to fight, even though it may imply aggressiveness or stubbornness on our part. These are attitudes we assume in a combat where we won't give up and will allow us to reaffirm our identity. Aries is a birth sign of pioneers; those who open a path so that others can follow.

The energy of Aries is primary and instinctive. This is demonstrated in every new stage of our lives, when we are not sure how we are supposed to react and instead behave spontaneously, letting our outbursts of energy to take over. It doesn't help to try to be logical or suppress this energy. Involving our thoughts and feelings we cannot assure success.

Aries gives us the chance to manifest its energy the way it is. It has a great potential that should come out naturally as the basis for further development. When we were learning to walk, we tried small steps, and more than once we fell and hurt ourselves. However, this is a part of our learning process and as children we tried once and again regardless of the consequences. Only with time and experience we became capable and confident of our own capabilities.

EXERCISES

It is possible that during the time you are working with Aries, aggression and hostility show up when you try to establish your territory. Be aware of these signs and work on them. Be firm in your decisions and manage aggression wisely. If you find yourself tense and angry try practicing a sport or working on a new project. Focus your energy constructively and creatively.

WEEK ONE

This is the beginning of the beginning. You will honor the energy of Aries by allowing it to manifest itself naturally. Search for your real identity and find what are the attributes or characteristics that define you. In the past, the first name of a person was followed by an attribute or profession that made him recognized by others in the community. Today we recognize these through family names. We can see many examples of these family names: like Hunter, Slater etc. Finding what would be your name at this moment, according to what you think, can define your identity. Remember that our occupation or profession is of great importance when we are defining who we are. Think how you would introduce yourself to a group if it were to be done by who you are, rather than by the given family name.

This week you will be playing with your name to find out what are the attributes you identify with. You could even choose a new name during this week and ask other people to call you by this name in order to try a new expression of your personality. Aries needs to manifest spontaneously and playfully.

WEEK TWO

The second week of Aries will be dedicated to define a space or territory for that identity you rediscovered during week one. This is a creative and concrete exercise related with your need to have physical space that is private and that you hold as your exclusive property. Organizing your closet, library or office desk, getting rid of old stuff and acquiring new free space are good ways to approach your identity and define which parts need a change.

Your new space, newly organized, can be marked with your name. If you have children, it is possible they are used to taking your things and your space. At this moment, you can establish some new limits that will allow you to define a new territory, exclusively yours.

WEEK THREE

Expand your limits. Think about imposing your identity in areas you share with other members of your family or group. For instance, if you have a wide garden that everyone in the family shares, you could choose a small area of it to set a tea table and chairs. Another good example of this expansion would be to change something in your car or install a new gadget you need when you travel long distances.

WEEK FOUR

If you practice a sport, try to beat your own record. You could also choose a physical or recreational activity where you can compete with others. Observe your own strength and physical capabilities. Find out how far you can go without hurting yourself. It is possible to go beyond the limits that your mind imposes on you.

Be aware of what you have achieved and how far you have gone during this week. Did you manage to keep your limits safe? Examine if you felt you failed and why. Write about the areas where you think you could not keep the limits, because this subject will be developing throughout the next birth signs, or the next year, when the sun touches Aries once more.

I love and value myself.

TAURUS

20th April – 20th May

Taurus: Earth, feminine, fixed.

Taurus represents what we value, from money to our physical body. It relates to all that is pleasant and comfortable. People born during the month of Taurus enjoy finding pleasure and comfort in all aspects of their lives. The search for pleasure is instinctive and not rational as it is directed towards natural enjoyment like a baby breastfed by his mother. At that moment the baby simply wants to satisfy an immediate and simple need. Our basic and primary needs are the ones that provide us with the greatest pleasure.

Although we look for a concrete and primary pleasure, the lesson Taurus offers is deeper: we must learn to value. In Aries we determined what our territory and limits were. When the sun comes to Taurus we have to look after this territory, find out its worth for us, and explore what we can do with it in order to utilize its resources. Suppose you just bought a piece of land in a place you wanted. That was Aries working. The next step responds to Taurus: it will make you think of a way to use this land to provide you with what you need to survive. It may be a place for holidays, where you can find the relaxation needed after a long working week; it can also be rented out so that others can enjoy it, or you could grow fruits or vegetables and sell them to earn a profit. In all cases, you assign a particular value to this property you own because of what you can gain from it. Likewise, you have to give a value to your identity, your capabilities, your body and every element that defines who you are.

Our body is our most important territory, asset or property. It is our vehicle in this planet and, therefore, we have to take care of it and nurture it properly. It is important to feed our body with an adequate diet according to its requirements. We should also exercise it daily, we must learn to breathe, so that it can acquire the right amount of oxygen and, most of all, we have to love and pamper our body. This also means we should stop attacking it with any kind of toxin or poison.

It is important to clarify that to value our bodies has nothing to do with working out to exhibit them. Many people believe that achieving a particular physical shape or structure is healthier and that this is what should be socially accepted or pursued. We have to understand that the body is not right or wrong by itself, but it is us who feel inadequate with it. We need to start accepting our physical structure and work to maintain our health with natural methods, always remembering that since it is our most valued asset, it is us who have to look after it. A physician can only help and guide us, but we hold the responsibility to take care of our bodies.

Our main asset (our bodies) also opens the access to another important issue: our self-esteem, and the way we earn self trust to face society and achieve our own goals. Depending on our self-esteem we assign a value to our capabilities, experience and knowledge and, when we offer these to others, we receive a payment for it. This payment must be concrete and valuable to us, as we are involved in an exchange of assets. Sometimes people feel that if they don't hold a degree, their experience and capabilities are less valuable than those of other professionals. It is not the task of society to determine what your value is. It is your obligation to clarify how valuable you are so that you become involved in a fair exchange of assets.

Taurus is related to the way we earn our living. Needless to say, our profession has a lot to do with earning money and the way we use our assets to earn it. The world's system imposes payment with a paper currency. However, many occupations are unfairly compensated as a result of an unfair social system. This is a good moment to evaluate whether we choose to support these values and the system they belong to, or if we can improve it by creating alternatives that provide a fair exchange for us and for others. In communities where money is scarce and people need to exchange their goods to survive, a barter system is coming back, giving them the possibility to create a different economy where they still can receive a material compensation for their work. This is just one example of the creative ways we could find so that our assets are valued while we also value other people's work.

Taurus reminds us that we should be truthful to those things we really care about. However, it is important to first examine if we have assigned the right value to our body, our knowledge, our capabilities and our enjoyment. Once we clarify how our priorities stand, we will advance quickly towards our goals because then it is easier to determine what are the assets we can spare, share or exchange to achieve what we want.

EXERCISES

WEEK ONE

This is a week to examine your body. As we mentioned, this is the most valuable asset you have and it would be a good moment to make sure everything is working properly. Visit your doctor for a check up if you haven't done it in a long time.

This is a week for body wellness and you could also go for a massage session. Remember that you love and care about your body. Another alternative would be to buy something that gives you pleasure and comfort. If the money you earn is not enough for this luxury, it could be a good opportunity to ask for a raise or analyze if you should price up your capabilities.

Take responsibility for yourself and be aware of your values and assets. Make a list of your priorities in life. This will give you the chance to understand yourself better and to realize whether you respect these regardless of society or if you might be assuming someone else's priorities and values rather than your own.

WEEK TWO

The second week of Taurus requires you to be aware of physical contact with others. In our current society, we have forgotten the importance this has as a tool to provide and acquire trust between human beings. With our children, we often overlook how physical affection makes up for a lot of unspoken words, and can help them to overcome emotional distance or distress. Pets are the best example of physical affection. Since they cannot use words with us, their demonstrations of love are physical, natural and truthful. This week might be a good moment to take care of a pet and connect with this natural love.

We all have the natural capability to show love and affection to others through physical contact. This week, try to hold more hands, hug more often, kiss more frequently and touch every one with love and care.

During this week you should also buy clothes or other personal items for yourself. However, make sure you spend only what you yourself have earned not your spouse's or family's money. If you have been saving for something in particular, analyze if this goal is truly important to you or if it actually belongs to someone else. Remember to identify what you really value.

WEEK THREE

Because you have analyzed your values and assets, this would be a good time to get rid of things you don't use or need anymore. Dispose of those possessions you have kept for no apparent reason. It could be a good time for a garage sale or to give away those things you found useless in this new stage of your life.

Since you are re-examining your possessions, you could also give sentimentally valuable things to members of your family. Memorabilia, photographs or jewelry are sometimes more appreciated by our children or family relatives than by ourselves because they will receive them as special gifts and treasure them accordingly.

You can also start gardening or cooking classes, learn about investments or taxes. These activities are related to Taurus and will help you to get in touch with its energy.

WEEK FOUR

You made some changes in your values and worked with physical affection. Now you should evaluate how others reacted towards these changes. This week will be dedicated to be aware of your own satisfaction and pleasure. Regardless of the reaction of others, feel comfortable and enjoy your changes. Expand this joy to your diet, body, work space and, if you feel that some comfort is missing, try to find a way to achieve it. If your office is not comfortable enough, maybe you could replace your chair, bring a few plants or photographs, change your desk, etc.

To enjoy simple pleasures in life is a fundamental ingredient to feel healthy. Many people agree that a feeling of joy in the present moment, regardless of the activity carried out, can make a big difference in the results. Remember to expand your pleasure and take your time, for instance, to taste your food and enjoy every minute of your lunch hour. This does not require you to take more time. Simply focus on the food you are eating and feel how it makes you feel better and satisfied.

I express and communicate who I am.

GEMINI

21st May – 20th June

Gemini: Air, masculine, mutable.

Gemini as an air birth sign relates to our need to express and communicate. It is a birth sign traditionally identified with quick and sharp intelligence and with people dedicated to commercial activities or traveling. These occupations suggest an exchange of energy. Take for instance the case of merchants in old times. They traveled buying and selling products they exchanged in every town they visited and their skill to calculate prices and bargain for goods required them to be sharp and quick. Bargaining became an art since they had to develop the capability to analyze fast and accurately if they could get a good profit out of any deal with their customers.

People from Gemini can be extremely quick and sharp with information, numbers and intellectual skills. However, due to the great amount of information they deal with, it is very seldom that they have the opportunity to deepen their knowledge beyond the evident. Imagine the World Wide Web. You can browse endlessly looking for information in any subject you choose. You will find abstracts and summaries about this information but often the outcome of your search is superficial and probably you would have to use another source of information or go thoroughly through each web page you search to ensure a deeper knowledge.

As we mentioned above, Gemini is energy that needs to be expressed and communicated. Thanks to its speed and sharpness it allows us the possibility to see the opposite side of any situation. This capability has to be used consciously to avoid conflict which would rapidly lead to mistrust when one side of the situation is favored against the other. Duality implies both sides or opposite sides of a situation and this view allows us to acquire knowledge that could serve others. In the case of journalists for instance, they may be the first ones finding out about situations that are relevant to all of us. They need to communicate this information quickly and accurately. However, sometimes, due to the speed required to keep up to date, their judgment is superficial and they end up producing wrong interpretations of reality.

To receive and communicate the information we get should be done in a way that focuses on one point instead of several. In Gemini we often fail to focus on one single point and rather choose to see a variety of possibilities that lead to confusion and superficiality. It leads us to avoid penetrating deeply the core of a subject. Gemini needs to find depth to overcome confusion. Once we start concentrating our energy in one basic point, the thought or message we want to express will flow clearly. This is the same process that writers and journalists need to go through. Once they choose a subject to write about, they need to unify concepts and relevant ideas in order to concentrate in one single reality, from which they can start a playful game of words and thoughts that will reach the minds of millions.

People with the energy of Gemini may have difficulties with communication and expression. Not only their voice or speech could be affected, they might find it hard to choose a way to communicate and convey how and what they feel and think.

Gemini's nature is to be able to see the opposite sides of any situation. It is required to experience both sides and learn to decide when both have been explored. But the decision has to be conscious. It requires us to realize that once we choose one side, we have to let go of the other. People living with someone from Gemini need to understand that duality is their nature and should choose one side to help them to take their own decisions.

EXERCISES

WEEK ONE

Every human being has polarity in himself. Accept seeing both sides of everyone. Our planet receives the light of the sun on one side, while the other side is dark. This process is the same we experience in our lives and it is important to accept it. You can see the positive and negative sides of your partner, relatives and friends. If you feel it is hard to accept this duality in the people you love, it would be a good moment to have a straight conversation to clarify and learn to accept that positive and negative have to be unified but, mostly, that they actually coexist in every one of us.

Choose someone you love and care about and make a list of positive and negative things about him or her. This is not to create a conflict, but to improve your relationship with that person. Once you communicate your feelings about this relationship, there will be a possibility to improve it, by being able to find the deepest reasons behind conflict. This practice should be done with joy and in a playful manner, always remembering it is not intended to express hidden anger towards others. Its aim is to learn to know each other with love and care.

WEEK TWO

The work you have been doing with the person you choose for the exercise on the first week will continue during this one. Find some activities you both find interesting, like conferences, exhibitions, concerts, etc. Once you agree on one you both like, pick different moments or days to go. Afterwards, sit together and share your thoughts and ideas about the same event. This will help you realize that, although we might be looking at the same thing, the view is different for each of us and it also has some common points to all.

To be responsible for our relationships also means to respect our partner understanding that there are differences that can be used to complement each other. It is also related to our need to understand that by being different we complete each other because we can share and exchange capabilities.

WEEK THREE

It is important that you become aware of the flow of thoughts constantly bombarding you. We all know it is difficult to stop them. However, they can be directed towards any particular subject instead of allowing our minds to wander uncontrollably. Be aware of how quickly you move from one idea or subject to the next one and concentrate on one at a time as part of your routines for Gemini.

The same way we will focus on our thoughts, will also require us to complete one task at a time, instead of leaving it to pick a new one. Choose a magazine or article you have been meaning to read or write a letter to a friend you have been thinking about for a long time. Do not suspend your task for later. Go from the beginning to the end of your task without interruptions.

WEEK FOUR

This is a good time to take a trip with a group of friends or family. Examine and observe silently how the relationships are within the group and between you and the others. Can you really accept positive and negative aspects from people surrounding you? If you find that you are short of tolerance, let your emotions take over your thoughts and search deeply for the real source of conflict.

Conflicts that cannot be resolved between the parts should be treated with the help of a professional or someone that you consider can give you a new perspective to sort out thesituation. In many cases you will discover that a third opinion provides a fresh view necessary to clarify thoughts in both parties.

I love Mother Earth. She nurtures and looks after me.

CANCER

21st June – 22nd July

Cancer: Water, feminine, cardinal.

Cancer energy is represented by what we consider to be our roots. Our home, family and ancestors relate to this birth sign, but in general all these can be grouped as a mother figure; a person who gave birth to us, helped us to grow and raised us. The influence of the environment where we grew up (language, race, cultural traditions, etc) is translated into this birth sign. Cancer is associated with the energy we received at birth and did not choose consciously. Cancer will be perceived as a natural energy in the beginning of our life, when it was our mother who showed us the traditions she followed.

As time goes by we realize that this heritage is not specifically ours and belongs to our race or group. As we grow up we meet other people, travel or exchange thoughts and opinions with other cultures and then we compare our own experiences with others, realizing that there are differences between all human beings and between cultures. People who carry the energy of Cancer will see this as a process that strengthens their need to come back to the first years of their childhood, or their memories of those times, when traditions, habits and customs provided security and protection.

Generally speaking, the energy of Cancer always looks for that "shelter" we thought we had when we were small and a mother figure provided a comfortable feeling of protection. The energy of Cancer is feminine and the sun, being a masculine figure, cannot express this energy as easily as it does on masculine birth signs. The energy of the sun is related to the identity of the individual and in Cancer the identity is provided by the family. Sometimes this does not allow an individual to grow by himself and a conflict appears as he would rather be identified by his own characteristics and not by his family or the community he belongs to.

During the last decades, the energy from Cancer expressed through the family has suffered as a consequence of changes in society and culture. Mothers have been driven to work outside the home and children are looked after by someone else. Regardless of the reason, mothers are not available all the time to care for their children and basic needs of love, care and security have lost their real value. Childhood should be the time when human beings receive constant assurance until they reach a stage where, by natural law, they are emotionally, physically and mentally mature enough to care for themselves.

There are stages in our lives when we require to be looked after for every necessity and other stages when we need our mothers to leave us on our own to develop independence and self-assurance. When the basic need of love and protection is not satisfied at the right moment, we could end up looking for satisfaction in areas where we think we would satisfy them. This unconscious search for the love and protection we did not get when needed, can lead us to consume or acquire all kinds of material goods, from food to objects we feel should satisfy this lack we have kept inside for a long time. For instance, when it rains I prepare hot chocolate to drink while sitting by the window. I immediately feel safe and protected because my mother used to prepare hot chocolate for me as I was afraid of storms. However, if the need for attention and security would have expanded from stormy weather to other instances where I felt worried or afraid, I could have used hot chocolate as a comfort food and even expanded it to other types of food, generating a relationship between my worries and my diet.

Traditions, habits or customs we acquired at home provide us with roots from which we take the nourishment we need. Imagine a tree: in the beginning, when it is small, it requires the soil to provide it with humidity, minerals and other elements necessary for its growth. After it grows it generates an independent ecosystem that already has the capability to keep moisture, produce seeds and reproduce and nourish others. However, the roots are still the most important part in the process of keeping its own balance. In our case, our roots are always a point of reference to remember our own identity and to understand where we come from. To know our roots and our past helps us to identify who we are, so that we can achieve clarity on who we want to become. When the grape seed understands what vines and grapes are, and that it will eventually arrive at that stage of development, it can become the best vine, and produce the best quality grapes, and even transform itself into the best quality wine.

EXERCISES

WEEK ONE

To remember your past, both good and bad, is an important task for this week. Look for the family album, find pictures of your childhood, your mother, grandparents, family meetings, the house where you lived and items from this time of your life.

Another good exercise for this week will be to come back to your past through people who shared your childhood and shaped your memories. You could visit your grandparents and ask them about you when you were small. You can also ask your mother to prepare you a meal you used to enjoy when you were a child.

WEEK TWO

There are always critical situations we remember from our childhood, sometimes related to pain or abuse by adults. Do not feel surprised if you examine one of these memories and find that you are still resentful toward someone you think was responsible for bad childhood memories. There could be hidden feelings you never discussed or mentioned to anyone regarding incidents with relatives or friends. This is the moment to resolve those feelings within yourself, by forgiving them and remember not to make the same mistakes with children close to you or with your own family.

To forgive is to accept that someone who acted ignorantly towards us probably did it because of his own circumstances or bad experiences in the past. When we forgive, we are able to detach and free ourselves from pain and suffering. Since you have been going through old things from your childhood, this will be a good moment to give away items that have lost sentimental value for you. You could even burn these items if they are attached to bad memories and as they burn you would transform negative energy into positive energy.

WEEK THREE

Recognize that what your mother provided you with implied her sacrifice and required her to postpone her own plans for later while you grew up. This was necessary for your growth and you should not feel guilty, but grateful. If at this moment of your life you were asked to make a sacrifice for your children's sake, it will be rewarded in the future when you look at them and see they are secure and have found their own ground.

If you are a good person, living a decent life, it could be because of the good work your parents did. As they age, they need you to give them love and care to reward them. Find out if they have a special wish you can grant them now and try to please them to show them that you are grateful for their sacrifice. Now you understand what it means to give up personal plans to provide others with a better chance in life.

WEEK FOUR

Dedicate this week to concrete issues related with your family, your home and your children. Home tasks you've been postponing should be done during this week. You can also try to share these activities and the work to be done with members of your family. If you have the chance to share more time with them, go camping or fishing, as these activities will help you release and enjoy the energy of Cancer.

Another good activity to carry out during this week is to cook with or for your family. A Sunday lunch for instance, could be a good opportunity to share with your relatives and your partner's relatives as well. Accept the differences between the members of both families as the union of two groups that belong to this planet. Be conscious about the fact that there are different races, groups and languages around the globe, and even though they differ from yours, they belong to the same family: humanity.

I am Love.

LEO

23rd July – 22nd August

Leo: Fire, masculine, fixed.

The energy of Leo should be used to recognize ourselves through our creativity and our creations. Leo leads us to create in order to recognize our individual identity beyond the limits of a family or social group. Imagine a family where the parents are active members of their company's union. As their child grows in this environment, his identity could be influenced by his parents' values and opinions. However, the child has the capability to use this same energy creatively when he grows up, not by belonging to a union himself, but by becoming professionally involved in labor politics. The identity and individuality that were born, and discovered their own territory in Aries, will be defined by the way they are expressed creatively in Leo.

Everyone recognizes the energy of this birth sign individually. However, to be creative or to manifest our Leo creativity can prove difficult. Often, if we feel afraid to express creatively, we end up identifying with others who dare to do it. A good example of this identification can be seen in teenagers, who "fall in love" with a movie star or popular celebrity. This happens during a time when a deep conflict arises: teenagers are in the process of discovering their own individuality and don't know how to express it yet, so they find in these idols the elements they identify with, and follow them. Somehow, these popular people dare to do successfully what the teenager wouldn't do for fear of judgment and failure.

The image we choose, or which we identify with on the outside, is a reflection of ourselves. When we realize that this image is inside us, we define our identity and can start to work creatively to build it up. However, an exaggerated search to define that same identity can make us self-centered, as the ego enjoys affirming itself at all times. Our real development and evolution happens when we express our individuality to be used for a common good, either in the family, group, or society at large.

The balance we need to find when we are defining our identity is related to the importance of exercising a particular role in our society. We should not look for an identity that repeats itself on the outside, or follows already explored paths. The lesson we have to learn with Leo is to express our own identity with our internal and intuitive force, so that it can take us to achieve our mission and to do what we have to do.

In a family with several children, it is possible to find characteristics from the parents in every child. Each one will have a particular combination of physical traits from the father and the mother, which makes them unique. We are singular and unique thanks to this particular combination that has taken place. Although these characteristics are identified with someone else in the family, the way they have been combined will not be repeated. The same happens with our psychological and emotional characteristics. These are also particular qualities that are combined in a specific way and therefore belong only to each individual. It is your individual responsibility to use them to let others know who you are.

Immaturity makes us choose stereotypes (movie stars, rock stars, models, successful entrepreneurs, political leaders) to imitate them and to avoid the responsibility of being ourselves. When we decide to be ourselves, we have to face approval, rejection and failure. Our identity shows to the group who we really are. Inevitably, there will be times of solitude when rejection occurs. This is the moment to acquire the strength to show and stand for our own truth, being creative. This means to find elements that balance harmoniously the expression of our individual identity and the identity of the group. In the tale of the Ugly Duckling, he begins his life with rejection and he wanders alone for a long time. But then, the time comes when he is accepted and recognized thanks to his real identity. Not trying to be a gracious duck, he turns into a beautiful swan.

EXERCISES

WEEK ONE

This is a good week to practice your favorite sport or start exercising in a gym. Look for an activity that makes you feel at ease and helps you to keep fit at the same time. Dancing, figure skating or aerobic exercises are examples of the activities you could practice during the first week of Leo.

To keep in touch with your physical image makes it easy to reinforce and strengthen your individuality when you accept that you are different from others. Being able to see who is in a better or worse shape than you is part of the task of locating yourself in a group and acknowledging your own strengths and weaknesses without being judgmental.

WEEK TWO

This is a good week to exercise your individuality in tasks you perform daily and find creative ways of improving the results of these routines. This is the power to individualize your work or occupation. Organize your workload, your activities and create alternative tasks. For instance, if you are in a managerial position, this is a good moment to delegate activities that normally you would do yourself. Start finding free time to pursue new ideas or to find new ways to perform old tasks. Organize your group so that it works more efficiently.

Creativity is a great force and you should be aware that this force exists in you. Be conscious about this capability to create by finding alternatives in your life. Choose to try new ideas and perspectives whenever you feel you are connecting with your creativity.

WEEK THREE

This is a good time to have great fun with your children or in an environment normally dedicated to children, such as an amusement park or a family movie. This will lead you to reencounter your inner child, enjoy simple pleasures and be thrilled by the possibilities offered every day. Be playful during the week, paying special attention to your capability to free yourself from adult structures. Give yourself the chance to enjoy every simple experience once again, just as you used to do it when you were a child.

WEEK FOUR

Examine and practice a hobby or activity you have abandoned for some time, either due to lack of time or because you just lost interest. Find a place where you can go and try this activity once more, socializing with people who share the same interest. Do not take this practice very seriously or set up goals for the future. Simply remember it is something you enjoyed and practice this attitude in as many areas of your life as possible to overcome obstacles joyfully.

I am healing light.

VIRGO

23rd August – 22nd September

Virgo: Earth, feminine, mutable.

When we see the sun passing through this birth sign, we have the opportunity to develop further the concept of who we are and what our identity is. It is here that we have to review and analyze the mistakes we have made while we were defining ourselves.

During the first stages (the time we see the sun moving from Aries to Leo), the main objective was to recognize and individualize ourselves in order to face the outside world, to connect with others and with society. Now the energy of Virgo pushes us to perfect the work we have done so far. Virgo gives you the opportunity to serve, cleanse and reorganize. Think of a factory: every day, raw material passes through different processes to be transformed into thousands of finished products ready to be used. However, if the mechanical system that supports the production fails at some stage, everything will be affected. Therefore, there are certain periods when the machinery passes through a check up and maintenance process in order to guarantee its efficiency. Although self-observation should be a constant tool for improvement and change, when the sun is passing through Virgo we arrive to a point where we have to review and examine our internal processes in order to identify where we have to focus our attention, and correct our mistakes so that we can continue our quest for evolution.

Virgo is also related to physical illness. It is our physical body who speaks up when something is wrong inside. It could be talking to us about a thought or emotion that has not been recognized consciously or that we have been afraid to confront. Our physical body will receive the information about this hidden or ignored feeling and will express it as an illness. In traditional Chinese medicine, internal organs also represent a particular energy as well as a positive and a negative emotion. When a patient's organ is affected, the doctor will also identify the corresponding emotion that could be involved in this physical illness.

The energy of this birth sign is directed to the detail and technique required by any occupation or career to achieve mastership. Anything produced around us is only completed once the details are finished. Before that, there will be elements that require attention and refinement before creation is concluded. This is the same process we fulfill individually and in society. To obtain a professional title for instance we go through rigorous examination. However, our pursuit for mastership continues after graduation and we access other courses and training to gain further experience and knowledge and refine our skills. Either individually or through other institutions, we assess again our capabilities until we achieve acknowledgement of our mastership in a subject.

The energy from Virgo can help us to draw attention towards detail and, at the same time, to use this capability to help and serve others with humility. However, a lack of awareness of Virgo energy can lead to extremes: people can become incapable of establishing limits between service and servility. On the other hand, to pick on details can become a source of rude criticism. Self-criticism can become relentless and criticism can become so obsessive that if it reaches the outside it may hurt others deeply.

To serve others we begin by understanding their importance. Then, we have to give them the best of ourselves to help them to grow, to develop and to face the outside world with a sense of transcendence and belonging to a totality. As in the example of the machinery we mentioned before, even the slightest failure of one single part can produce mistakes in the whole production. Therefore, we care for every single piece and remember it belongs to a bigger system that requires its perfect performance to function.

It is possible that people from Virgo keep routines or structured thoughts. However, life will teach them that surprises and unexpected events can change these structures suddenly and in this birth sign they will have to learn to be flexible and adapt to changes.

EXERCISES

WEEK ONE

Recognize the importance you assign to structures and routines. Make a list of your daily routines, remembering the time you spend on each of them and the sequence you keep. This is a good week to break these routines and examine how flexible and adaptable you are to new procedures and structures. Flexibility will help you to release nervous tension.

WEEK TWO

Ask close friends how they see you and what they think about the way you communicate your opinions. Accept outside criticism with humility and be accessible to others. This does not mean you should change the way you are. Instead, you must understand that everyone is entitled to their own opinion and it is impossible for you to please everyone. Analyze if any criticism could be used to improve a particular aspect of your life, or if you feel fine the way you are. You may find you are comfortable with yourself and therefore are unwilling to change for others.

WEEK THREE

This is a good time to pay attention to details from your life you might have considered irrelevant. Vague allergies, stomach upsets, headaches at certain times of the day, all might be the symptoms of something else you have not taken the time to examine. These do not necessarily mean a hidden physical condition. Constant headaches, for instance, could be related with a state of anxiety you are not correcting and, more than medicine, your body might be asking you for more hours of sleep, or to exercise to release tension. Analyze your symptoms and see if they are in any way connected with your routines or something that has been bothering you for some time. Be conscious about the perfect connection between your body and your mind.

WEEK FOUR

To learn something on your own could be an excellent practice to release the energy of Virgo. Instead of looking for a class or teacher on the outside, explore your own capability to teach yourself if there is a particular subject you have been meaning to learn about.

This could also be a good time to start a class that can help you achieve a professional specialization. Finding specific literature about your profession and studying it during your free time could be another option. A trip to the library or bookstore will provide entire collections of manuals and literature on every subject.

I am harmony, beauty and peace.

LIBRA

23rd September – 22nd October

Libra: Air, masculine, cardinal.

The search we go through with the energy from Libra is to reconcile and balance the opposites. This quest is directed at finding harmony, beauty and balance in everything we do, especially in reference to our relationships. In Libra we need to connect with the other, giving and receiving energy in a harmonious, balanced and beautiful way. This energy leads us to abandon our personal and individual development to start a new learning process on how to complete ourselves with the other. During the first six birth signs we were learning to know and develop ourselves from an individual identity. In Libra, the learning changes focus. The other, our partner, friend or opposite, will provide the part we need to become whole.

In all aspects of our lives where we look for harmony, balance and beauty there is completion between the opposites. We might have a beautiful table, but it will not be complete unless we find the chair to sit in front of it. In our relationships, we all have wonderful qualities to offer to our partner. Likewise, there are wonderful qualities from our partner and we need to find our own balance. It is also important to realize that balance does not mean to find someone exactly like you. Instead, it is your opposite who completes you. If you are shy and introverted, most probably you will need the extroverted and outgoing nature of your partner, so that he or she can provide you with that particular social quality to face the outer world. At the same time, this extroverted partner will find in you a person able to listen and observe quietly to provide an alternative view.

The harmonious expression of Libra is usually located on one side of the scale, provoking in the other a sudden imbalance. To search for harmony often leads to situations of aggression, rage and negative emotions, especially when the internal evolution we had to go through during the first six birth signs was not experienced adequately. It is necessary to be clear about ourselves, and to know where we direct our objectives before starting to relate with others. When you know that the ground where you stand is safe and feel secure and determined, the other can help you to walk in company but with freedom, without competition, neither pushing nor pulling you.

Marriage is a constant competition if we have not solved the conflicts of our ego. We either try to be better than our partner, or to change them into what we think is right. Seldom can we find a couple where partners completely respect each other's freedom. If we can accept ourselves the way we are (recognizing our strengths and weaknesses), we can accept others for what they are, and only then we will be able to see that polarity and opposites exist also inside of us.

It is important to understand we will always need the other to manifest ourselves in a more complete way. We will always need positive and negative because when they are in touch, the possibility of growth becomes a reality. To grow, we will always need the other part that can make us whole. The same way positive and negative poles get in touch and produce electricity, each person needs to complete with an opposite who has the missing part. This enables every one of us to become whole and transform this energy into something concrete that serves others.

EXERCISES

WEEK ONE

During this week observe and take your partner's place. This is the way we understand what the other's view is. Imagine you are talking with someone face to face inside a room you don't know. You are able to see what is behind your partner; the color of the wall, the furniture, the curtains and so on. Likewise, your partner can see what is behind you. However, neither of you would know what is behind you unless your partner describes it. By integrating both views you can have a complete perspective of the whole room.

If you are passing through difficult times in a relationship, this is a good time to seek therapy or counseling. A third person who can observe and analyze objectively the ideas, thoughts and needs of both partners is of great help when we have trouble understanding our opposite to find a solution through harmony and creativity.

If you have difficulties in your social interactions it is time to face them and find help through seminars or workshops.

WEEK TWO

To continue with the work you have been doing during the first week, this is a good moment to take responsibility for the changes you have to make in what refers to relationships and society. It is important to become aware of the mistakes made in the past, being honest with yourself. When someone does not understand us, we have to accept that it is because we have not made our point clear, but also it is not necessary to convince others of the righteousness of our arguments. Be open to discussion with the person you face; your spouse, friend, co-worker or anyone you relate with.

WEEK THREE

Take time to schedule entertaining activities with your partner or spouse. For example, go with other couples to the movies or dancing. Another good choice would be to invite them home for dinner. It is important to observe other couples to understand that there are opposites in every relationship and that the members always have to complement each other. This practice will also give you the chance to see that other couples face similar conflicts to yours. Often, casual conversations between couples would help everyone to realize that it is common to all relationships to face difficult times. Conflicts are useful to reach balance and completion when we have the right attitude. Love and good will are a must.

WEEK FOUR

During the month of Libra you faced your partner and evaluated many issues related to conflicts existing between both. Thanks to the practices carried out during the previous weeks, you are ready to analyze if your partner is the person you are willing to spend your life with. Ask yourself if you really share with them in freedom, accepting each other for what you are and support each other in your personal lives, willing to commit to share more intimate issues. If during this evaluation you realize that your partner is not completing you, accept the reality of being alone to mature and grow in solitude, taking with you what you have esperienced living with your partner. You may feel the need to finish your relationship, but make sure it is a separation in good terms and that time will decide whether it will be definitive or just until both of you are ready to be together, once objectives are clearer and personal needs are satisfied.

If you realize your partner is the person who really completes you and that both are sharing your lives with a free spirit, this is a moment to materialize the relationship. To create something together is to make a statement that confirms that you are willing to grow and evolve as a whole. A simple task like redecorating your bedroom or creating a new, common space for both of you will help you as a couple to remember this commitment.

I am light of transformation.

SCORPIO

23rd October – 21st November

Scorpio: Water, feminine, fixed.

The deep feelings and emotions move the energy of this birth sign. Any person with a birth chart that shows the sun and/or planets in Scorpio, or an important position for this birth sign, will experience emotions in a deeply moving and transforming way. This energy makes us merge with the other. Deep feelings are like an image of a pond where all elements (water, soil, grass, plants, insects, etc) are combined in a dark environment that helps to transform and generate new species.

The energy of Scorpio demands transformation, regeneration. Crisis and deep change will be a natural consequence of what was primitive, ignored or has not worked out in the past. Scorpio is like a silkworm that starts its life crawling on the soil and passes through hardship and growth before locking itself in a cocoon, to finally emerge as a beautiful butterfly once the transformation is finished.

Scorpio energy leads us to a need to know how to control and dominate the environment. When this doesn't happen, like the scorpion, we tend to sting ourselves, preferring to die before giving in. Sex and power show the energy of Scorpio as a birth sign, and when we want to control our partner, it is normally reflected in our sexual behavior: if there is something we don't like or cannot change, we tend to walk away from the relationship ignoring the fact that we are denying ourselves the chance to enjoy shared pleasures because of our search for control and domination.

The energy of Scorpio is manifest in us when we feel in crisis. When we are falling into a deep, dark hole, panic and anxiety take over because we fear the unknown. This, however, is the moment to adapt ourselves to a new situation (somehow against our will), since we have to leave our comfort zone and adapt to the changes. We will have to reach deep inside us to find capabilities and talents we thought we did not have and they will appear naturally, showing us we can do things we thought impossible. This is the perfect moment to make a deep and decisive change, where we trespass the boundaries of our known world to find something new and meaningful.

To transform a crisis means to remove all that is negative to turn it into something valuable. Alchemy talked about converting any metal into gold. In old times, alchemists experimented with primary substances looking to convert them into something of high power. In this birth sign, the deepest and darkest aspects from us can be turned into a treasure we never thought we had. The majority of stories of greatly successful people have involved situations of pain and crisis before victory and achievement. For a person who loses all his money and possessions, finding himself in a crisis, life will take him instinctively to find new horizons. And from his own new discovered talents, a new possibility will raise for alternative strategies to achieve what he wants.

EXERCISES

WEEK ONE

This is a moment to start a cleansing process from the inside. You can start a diet or fasting routine to cleanse your negative emotions. Look for help from a professional to acquire a healthy discipline during this week. Also, make sure you get the rest and sleep necessary to reduce your levels of stress. You might have revealing dreams. Don't forget to write them down and, given the chance, try to find out their meaning.

Massage is an option to find relaxation. The objective of these practices is to release tension and anger you have accumulated over a long period of time without having had the opportunity to express them. Very often, these emotions account for physical and psychological states that we cannot control or understand.

WEEK TWO

During this week you can deepen your knowledge about your most intimate self. If you have realized there are emotional conflicts that need to be resolved, analyze if you need help from a professional. This is a good moment to dive into your consciousness and find out the real reasons and fears behind those conflicts. Before sorting out any situation, it is necessary to identify where the conflict lies.

Search in your intimate relations for a deep connection with your partner. Give in totally and from your heart, when you are together.

WEEK THREE

Visit a place from your childhood where you can find a spiritual connection with your past. If as a child you were taken to a special place by your grandfather, for instance, try to visit this place again and get in touch with the emotions the place brought to you at first. Find a silent spot to bring your deepest emotions to the surface.

You can also visit your grandparents' or family grave. When you face the meaning of death, you have the chance to let go of the past, remembering that to live is to be here and now.

WEEK FOUR

Through this month you reviewed several emotional and personal issues. From all that surrounds you (and you found negative at first), find the positive side and transform negative emotions into a challenge to reach a higher point in your life. Imagine yourself in a rainy day. You have to go somewhere but your car is broken, you cannot find a taxi and everything seems to be wrong. However, you can give yourself the chance to walk under the rain and get in touch with the wonderful feeling of the raindrops touching your skin, while feeling the wet soil and the music created with the presence of nature. If you can bring this transformation to all situations of your life, you will find the most precious treasure that exists inside of all human beings: love and enjoyment of life.

I am truth and expansion.

SAGITTARIUS

22nd November – 21st December

Sagittarius: Fire, masculine, mutable.

Sagittarius has the energy of a born searcher. It will look for depth and meaning in all that surrounds it and the inspiration for this search is initially intellectual. However, it looks for dimensions that trespass boundaries. It is common to find people from Sagittarius who travel often and work in foreign countries. They also go beyond the obvious because they are ultimately looking for the truth to widen their knowledge on every subject or fact of life.

Like other mutable birth signs, duality and polarity can create conflict in Sagittarius. It is hard to find the middle point between two opposites or acknowledge duality and experience it in a comprehensive or wholesome way. There are two parts inside ourselves: one is a human part that makes us emotional and passionate and the other is internal and spiritual, leading us to connect with the depths of the universe and the faith in a superior being. To accept both parts of ourselves and combine them is not easy and often leads to inner turmoil. When we go to the movies, we can watch a film on the big screen either focusing on the aesthetical part of the production or on the deep message the story holds. However, we really discover the magic of the movie once we manage to combine both sides. The depth of the story and the beautiful way it can be depicted stimulates our senses and our emotions.

In Sagittarius we must find a connection with that spiritual part of us and translate its existence into our daily lives. It requires us to accept that spirituality does not mean a perpetual mystical state that follows the laws of a religion. Instead, we should understand and feel that we belong to a totality and must adjust to it like a piece of a puzzle that belongs in an exact place to accomplish the universal plan. To achieve this, we first must find the deep truth of who we are. There is a story about a Zen master who attained enlightenment. At that precise moment, all he had to say was: "oh wonderful miracle; I can chop wood, I can get water from the well". Spirituality is nothing else but to be aware of our own reality and accept the presence of a superior being in every moment of our daily lives.

Our first step towards an encounter with spirituality happens in Sagittarius. Many times in life we find ourselves doing things we did not consciously choose, yet these seem to flow easily and produce great results without much effort. This happens when we accept to be channels for a truth that is beyond us, and we become vehicles of that force to manifest itself, helping others as much as it helped us.

EXERCISES

WEEK ONE

Take your time to enjoy a walk alone or a trip to an open place close to nature. A natural park or a forest will be perfect for this practice. Connect with your inner self and create an internal dialogue where you can think and feel your own reality. This will lead you to discover your real needs. Listen to your heart and analyze your thoughts to find your own truth.

WEEK TWO

What you found inside yourself last week should be focused creatively during this week. Be deeply sincere with yourself and with others and define in a simplified way where you are standing. If your definition passes through something personal, familiar or work-related, take those concepts you clarified into a creative expression of your own philosophy of life. Sometimes even a song can hold a deep truth we identify with and provide us with a simple philosophy of life we can carry in our hearts.

WEEK THREE

Once more, you should find a natural open space where you can go often and feel at ease. Choose a place where you feel comfortable. Again, natural parks, open fields and places where you can get a great view or enjoy a wide landscape will provide you with an insight on the connection existing between man and nature. It is important also that you become aware of the trip itself, preparing things with anticipation and realizing the sequence of events as they develop between planning the trip and actually reaching the place. We pass through this same process when we choose a spiritual quest. In reality, both trips are more or less the same.

WEEK FOUR

If you hold a particular spiritual belief, or if you feel the need to become identified with a particular philosophy or religion, this week you should look for a place where you can deepen your knowledge and feelings regarding this issue. A temple, school or education center are good examples of places where you can find answers to your questions on philosophy or religion. You can also buy a book on the philosophy you want to study if it helps you to identify your own philosophy of life.

I am spiritually protected and sustained.

CAPRICORN

22nd December – 19th January

Capricorn: Earth, feminine, cardinal.

The energy from Capricorn talks about the basic structure that represents where we find support. From there, we shape our lives up. Capricorn also represents time as a framework or boundary that provides us with a reference to develop and evolve.

A structural base supports us and gives shape to the situations we face in life. Laws and norms are also a structure. Their existence is a requirement for a community or society to work responsibly and fairly. A building needs a strong framework to sustain a great amount of weight and allow people to share the space in a secure way. Likewise, societies require a common framework that sustains its members safely.

Capricorn will help us to understand our structures so that they can serve as a foundation from which we will define what we will build around them. Any learning process has certain structural bases. Once we understand and know them, we will achieve further awareness. We will master these bases to shape any circumstance we face. When an engineer builds a house, he knows that its building will require a foundation and a frame to be sustained. But once the base has been built properly, the shape, color and distribution of the space of the house will be different and individual. As humans we share the same framework: our bones. However, our common structure is covered and the outer layer makes us individual and unique.

Capricorn always looks toward the highest place, the top. Capricorn is constant, reserved, careful and methodical. It takes its time to develop safely so it can reach the highest position, but it has the risk of being trapped by its own structures. Many people from Capricorn tend to be ambitious and structured and they may ignore or hide parts of themselves that are basic to achieving a complete development. If what they try to avoid are their emotions and feelings, it is life which demonstrates with time that these are just as important as other achievements. At that moment, when emotions and feelings are brought to the surface, all structures break down. To work with this energy, one must know one's structures and accept them. But also acknowledge that in the world of emotions and feelings laws are shapeless. Love towards another person can make us forget social and religious conventions. There are times when a conflict appears between people from different races or religions. At that moment, structures must become flexible instead of breaking up or they risk destroying a whole creation.

To reach the top of a mountain we have to develop a serious discipline and basic training. Then we can try to climb up to the top. However, even though we might have the training and perhaps experience, we must always be flexible enough to accept the fact that conditions cannot always be in our favor and we should postpone our goals until the time comes when we know our efforts will be worthwhile.

Flexibility is not the only lesson of Capricorn, but also the capability to enjoy life and have fun. Sometimes a task might be very serious and should be taken with responsibility. However, this does not imply that we have to lose our ability to enjoy life and be happy while we work at it.

EXERCISES

WEEK ONE

List your structures. Ask others to provide you with examples about routines and structures they can see in you. This exercise will make you aware of the laws, norms and routines you have already acquired without noticing. If you feel the list is not complete, write down those structures which your friends and people around you have not noticed.

Take the opportunity to be flexible once you recognize your rules, laws and structures. Observe your feelings and emotions while you follow them.

WEEK TWO

Take time to pay attention to the way you look. Find out if you could change the way you dress or comb your hair just to break up a structure you face daily. It doesn't require a dramatic change in your looks or wardrobe, simply a slight variation that makes you feel different, even if others don't notice it.

WEEK THREE

Disorganize your closet, office drawers or any other place where you keep your belongings and organize it again, finding a new way to systematize your space.

Another good task for this week is to write down what you feel, even if you find it difficult to express, and be responsible to accept your feelings. Be aware of the essence of those feelings beyond the form and appearance.

WEEK FOUR

This week you can visit a place high up in the mountains, or a silent cave. The task here will be to walk towards a high place that will be held as a goal. This walk should be silent and alone to allow you to get in touch with your feelings and emotions, and bring to the surface thoughts and memories that might have been ignored in the past.

I am the essence of someone different and special.

AQUARIUS

20th January – 18th February

Aquarius: Air, masculine, fixed.

Aquarius is identified as the birth sign of inventors and visionaries, who can anticipate time and offer amazing advances to civilization. The sun crossing Aquarius gives us the chance to look for creative alternatives we have overlooked and teaches us what destiny means. Inventions like the airplane and the telephone (both related with the element air, where Aquarius belongs) required from their creators a capability to recognize that they could see reality in a different and individual way. They also faced their destiny by accepting to be channels to materialize knowledge that belonged to humanity.

Finding our destiny and being responsible for our individual differences, means following our nature: a flower knows it is a flower and does not pretend to be a tree. Neither will it try to stop being a flower. Our nature is often covered by social conventions, group pressure and also by our self-centeredness. We will have to remember that we are different and have individual characteristics that belong only to ourselves.

Aquarius gives us a mental and intellectual strength that can be used positively. However, we turn it against ourselves. As in a storm, where we perceive a time difference between the lightning and the sound of the thunder, in Aquarius our thoughts have great speed and we mentally grasp more than we can actually take in on the emotional and physical level.

Although the nature of Aquarius belongs to the world of ideas and superior knowledge, we have to reach a point where that highly intellectual knowledge is brought into a concrete level in a way that is practical and easy for everyone to reach. This is the same story humanity has faced with the examples of the airplane and the telephone. Today we can communicate with everyone around the globe and traveling by plane we can go to the other side of the world in less than twenty-four hours. It took time and effort, but ideas were brought into a material level where they were shaped and tested beyond the world of thoughts and imagination. They became a concrete part of our physical reality.

Many people go through life feeling they are different and they express it by choosing an unconventional look, joining groups or sects and even aggressively imposing their way of life. It would be useful to examine if they really feel free. In fact this is not an expression of real individuality, nor does it accomplish the task of being responsible for their differences. In Aquarius it is necessary to learn the difference between rebelliousness and genius. To rebel aggressively to break a structure proves useful if we are going towards a change where we can see facts from a different point of view and decide to approach the situation in an original and new way. This is different from rebelling without knowing the reasons behind the need to change. Teenagers, the natural rebels, need to break the structures from their families to achieve self assurance. They choose different ways to rebel: adopting abusive and disruptive behavior or finding ways to reach independence and creating alternative targets to direct their energy.

When we recognize our nature, we achieve the freedom to accept what is in store for us. This is the truth Aquarius shows us. When we become responsible for our individuality, we can face change and accept it as part of our mission in this planet and towards humanity.

EXERCISES

WEEK ONE

This week you will explore your creative potential. Use your inclinations and abilities to express what you perceive as your nature. Revealing yourself can be materialized through handicrafts, arts, sports, etc. The important issue during this week is that you choose something unconventional to feel different from the groups you belong to. If you have a hobby or discipline, this will be the moment to dare to practice it in a different way, or change it into something you might have wanted before, but thought it would not be appropriate.

Another way to express yourself is by changing your appearance. Color your hair, wear the clothes you did not dare to wear before, or change routines related to your personal care. These are just examples of the practice you will carry out this week. Be aware that you are provoking this change intentionally and accept responsibility for the consequences it will bring.

WEEK TWO

During the first week you have chosen a creative way to express difference and individuality. This week you will carry on this practice, regardless of comments and observations from people around you. Judgmental criticism may be difficult to bear, but will prove to help you to be responsible for your own individuality as well as to respect others' ideas.

Give yourself the chance to observe your previous behavior as it is reflected by others. Without understanding or knowing the reasons behind their behavior we often judge other people and establish a moral code which we consider to be the right one.

WEEK THREE

In the last two weeks, difference and individuality were exercised in order to help you feel comfortable and assured of your own identity. This week you will communicate to others what you feel and think in a different and original way. You can look for meetings or groups to discuss issues you are interested in. Take advantage of these and express your own ideas and thoughts without feeling afraid of showing who you really are.

WEEK FOUR

After three weeks of intense work, it is time for a reward. Choose a physical activity you can enjoy close to nature and practice it during this week. Hiking is recommended as Aquarius controls the calves, but any physical activity will work as a filter, to transform all emotions brought out during the past weeks. You will have the opportunity to observe your emotions as manifestations of your inner self. These were helping you to grow. Although you might have felt ignored, rejected or mocked, these emotions are part of accepting your individuality.

I am the Universe.

PISCES

19th February – 20th March

Pisces: Water, feminine, mutable.

Pisces can be compared to the expansion represented by the ocean. We perceive the ocean as a vast body of water where life has its origins. When we face the ocean we cannot find limits. It is a great landscape our eyes find immense. Pisces is the birth sign that represents this immensity; the vast landscape that makes us feel small and incapable of covering the extent of humanity without feeling we are about to leave the limits of our body.

Pisces belongs to the water element that identifies emotions. However, these emotions are not contained in the water of a lake or the flow of a river. Rather, we would think of Pisces like the depths of the oceans, where a sound can travel for great distances and be heard by sensitive beings like dolphins. When our emotions are deep we can have access to this same process: our emotions can be transmitted through great distances to be felt or perceived by our beloved ones even if they are physically far from us.

We should always think of everything that surrounds us and forms our environment as an ocean of vibrations. The waves surround us. They affect us and we can affect them, since there is a subtle weaving between all human beings that goes beyond individual differences or boundaries. Thoughts, feelings and actions from us have an effect in our environment and when we are not aware of that, they can imply a great help or a great confusion.

Imagine music as a particular kind of wave. It can have a relaxing effect in the people when it is soft and balanced. Likewise when it is loud and rhythmic, it produces a corresponding reaction in people exposed to it. When we listen to a soft violin playing, the sound seems to go straight to the heart, while drums are felt in the abdomen. These are examples that can be associated to the way emotions can directly affect our environment and, therefore, affect us. We might not be able to recognize or perceive the emotional energy around us at all times, but we can be sure it will have an effect on us, just as we will produce a change in our environment depending on our particular emotional energy.

To be aware of the connection between ourselves and humanity is not necessarily a profound and ethereal experience. It can be translated into our daily lives understanding thoughts, feelings and actions of others and being aware of our own. For instance, people who drive and drink are unaware of the danger it implies not only for themselves, but also for others as their capabilities to react to an unexpected situation are impaired. By understanding (and avoiding) this situation, we are becoming aware of our connection with humanity and we are consciously accepting our responsibility towards others.

When we look for a higher level of thought, emotion and action, we are touching a greater consciousness: the consciousness of humanity. This is the labor wise people from different religions and civilizations have done through the ages. Prayers, mystical secret practices and meditation have brought to earth this contact with Divine Inspiration and it is available to all of us the moment we become aware that we have Divinity inside us and are connected with it at all times.

In the depths of the oceans everything is perceived with a higher intensity. Likewise, people from Pisces can have a tendency to be extremely generous and sometimes experience an exaggerated sensitivity towards others, where there is a total surrender and boundaries between the self and others disappear. This transcendent sensitivity towards humanity surpasses the limits of the individual. It can be understood when we think for instance of a catastrophe in a remote place and it worries us. When we watch the news, somehow we feel the pain and anguish of the people passing through this situation. Every time there is an oil spill in the ocean we all feel it is a betrayal for us as humans, because our environment is affected and we understand that this will affect all of us at some point in time.

Pisces can connect us with universal understanding. However, if we fail to connect with Pisces' energy properly, we turn to avoidance and lose contact with reality. Drugs, alcohol, tobacco, religious fanaticism and the inability to foresee danger in high risk sports are examples of this avoidance. In essence, when we choose any of these activities or substances and overlook the danger implied in our choice, we are looking for a way to destroy the physical limits that sometimes we feel are trapping us. These activities or drugs seem to erase these boundaries, allowing us to perceive a subtle contact with Divinity. But since this connection is not real, we are only connecting, once again, with our ego and avoidance.

In our daily life, an excess of sacrifice makes us believe we are good people, while in reality we are looking for selfish rewards, without real surrender. Often people use sentences like "I am a very kind human being, yet I suffer so much" or "I am very spiritual and because of that sometimes people take advantage of me". These statements are not the result of real surrender, but rather a need for recognition. Real sacrifice and surrender are painless. We have inner emotions that allow us to understand that when we surrender, we will be rewarded by the universe, not by actual friends or family. In Pisces we are penetrating the subtle weaving of vibrations and threading it, and expanding our connection with the universe.

EXERCISES

WEEK ONE

To say what we think and feel, and express it through dance, music or simply by recognizing our real self in our emotional area, is important while we receive the energy from Pisces.

During this week, remember all your past experiences with water. Memories from trips to the beach, swimming and in general your feelings about the water will be important. Write down any particular event that happens to you during this time, that you feel is related to your emotions. If you live near the ocean, this is a good time to pay a visit. It is also important, while connecting with these emotions that you tell the people you love what your feelings are towards them.

It is possible that you will receive unexpected phone calls or news from friends or family you have not seen in a long time. Take this opportunity to get in touch with them and express those feelings you never dared to share with them. This task is not easy, but to work with emotions has never been. Give yourself the chance to connect consciously with your emotions.

WEEK TWO

The second week of Pisces will be dedicated to expressing emotions which we have locked inside us. During the first week you started to connect with those feelings and week two will be the time to bring out the emotions you hide.

The deepest emotion we have is love and, as humans, it relates to our bodies. Sexual intercourse should be considered a sacred activity where one gives in from the heart and surrenders with the body to give and receive pleasure. Look for a space to create an emotional connection with your partner. The deepest emotions can be expressed physically, and sexual intercourse should allow you to merge into one feeling, being aware that love is the essential energy of the universe and that through our sexuality we have a human way of expressing it. Spirit and body are not separated. They should merge in each of us as one single force.

WEEK THREE

The music you prefer represents a part of your identity. Most of the time, our taste for music is related to our generation and how we felt during the time that music was popular. During this week you should explore your connection with your favorite music in order to understand consciously your connection with humanity through your generational group.

The music your parents used to play when you were small certainly relates to you as it brings memories of your childhood. Sadness or happiness will characterize these moments and, by now, it is possible for you to identify the reasons that associate particular moods with those melodies. This week find the real feelings brought by the music you listen to, and identify the ideals and philosophy you associate with it.

WEEK FOUR

The month of Pisces has brought you a deeper contact with emotions. These are not personal emotions. Rather they relate to you as a member of humanity and as such, you should commit to a common cause or goal. We need love, care, nurture and tenderness, and these needs are common to all human beings. There could be a place near you where you can fulfill these needs for others and feel capable of serving others when the suffering is overwhelming.

You can also follow a good cause you feel is worthwhile. Remember that the best help you can provide is your energy and that it can be given in several ways. The basic task here is to become aware of your connection with humanity and the important role you play in it. Unselfish surrender to an ideal will give you the possibility to feel that everything you give away will be given back to you.

When I become the Ocean
I can reach every corner of the Universe
And I feel what you feel,
And what every other creature feels,
Because there are no limits between us.
We are One.

JOURNAL
—OF THE—
JOURNEY

ARIES

BE YOUR OWN WARRIOR. FIGHT YOUR OWN FIGHTS.

Suggestions for the month of Aries

- Being a pioneer in any area of expertise relates with the energy of Aries.
- This is a good time to become a guide. You can bring a group of people to explore a place you know well.
- The energy of Aries can be symbolized in nature by places where people compete with each other to win.
- The Grand Canyon is a good example of the energy of Aries in our planet.

Notes for reflection

1. Our identity is like a photograph of ourselves. However, it always reflects what we want to show others about us. To understand the way you visualize yourself in the meditation, remember with honesty how you felt while repeating the phrase for Aries. Did you feel self assured or insecure?
2. Accidents and mistakes should not be considered negative. In fact, they hold the very important role of showing you failure so that you can attain success.
3. What is your territory?

TAURUS

ENJOY YOUR BODY.

Suggestions for the month of Taurus

- To work the soil is related to Taurus' energy. Wine making and agriculture are good examples of activities associated with this birth sign. Copper craftsmen also hold a relation with the energy of Taurus.
- Taurus always knows the value of things.
- Sensuality is a natural quality of Taurus. It is expressed through the constant search for pleasure and comfort on every activity in life.
- The energy of Taurus can be found in prairies and valleys, where we can see great extensions of green pastures and gentle wind. Wherever the energy of Taurus is manifested, we will want to rest on the ground, relaxed and happy.

Notes for reflection

1. What do you really value? Your values are not subject to social approval. Remember they belong to you and therefore it is important to identify them clearly so that you can work for them.
2. Do you enjoy what you do? It shows when you feel comfortable and satisfied with yourself, because you take pleasure from the simple things in life.
3. Your skin is the largest organ of your body. Caress it.

GEMINI

COMMUNICATE WHATEVER THOUGHTS COME TO YOU. YOU ARE A MESSENGER OF THE GODS.

Suggestions for the month of Gemini

- Journalists, communicators, merchants, people related with commercial activities and also thieves are traditionally associated with the energy of Gemini.
- Short trips, business trips and goods exchange are activities from Gemini.
- Speech and expression as well as breathing are influenced by the energy of Gemini.
- The nature of Gemini is easily identified in our cities and specially bookshops. Any place where our curiosity can be satisfied is manifesting the energy of Gemini.

Notes for reflection

1. Is it difficult for you to decide between two options? To choose means you are ready to take control. To divide your attention between options will make it more difficult to find your real identity and to define what you really expect from life.

2. Information is always an asset. However, we should always be aware that the information we collect should be used, interpreted, shared and deepened to have a real value.

3. You can have as many activities in your life as you want, and be successful in all of them. However, do not forget to analyze if they are all important and necessary, or if perhaps you are using them to avoid what you really need to face.

CANCER

FIND IN YOUR ROOTS THE NOURISHMENT THAT SUSTAINS YOU.

Suggestions for the month of Cancer

- Nutrition and nurture are related to Cancer. The essence of Cancer is manifested on the image of a mother. Someone who nurtures and protects a child and also passes into him the history of the family, the group or the race.
- People from Cancer are extremely attached to their families often having many children of their own.
- Relaxing during a rainy day, perhaps in a warm cozy place and looking through a window could bring about the feeling of Cancer's energy.

Notes for reflection

1. What are you looking for when you eat? Besides the biological need, are you expecting to feel secure and protected? Clarify where your needs are. Often we eat more if we feel stressed. We can also be deeply affected in our eating habits when we don't know how to face certain situations. Be aware that you cannot exercise control on such instances either by eating or starving.
2. There is a time for everything. Never resent your present situation. Remember there will be a time when that will be over.
3. Forgive your family for those mistakes they made with you when you were a child.
4. Traditions, family values, inheritance and cultural background are part of you, but you are an adult and if these traditions or beliefs are obsolete, you are responsible for changing and adapting them to the present situation, so that they can represent something important for your own children.

LEO

THE PATH OF THE HERO IS TO BECOME HIMSELF.

Suggestions for the month of Leo

- Leo represents the knight or hero who goes through life fulfilling heroic deeds.
- People from Leo are normally good directors or managers organizing activities to achieve a goal. Jewelers, cardiologists, actors and presidents have the energy of Leo in their careers.
- The landscape of Leo will always have a bright sun shining or will be represented by a palace full of light and brightness.

Notes for reflection

1. Are you authentic? Can you show who you really are in front of everyone?
2. Take daily activities with a playful spirit. Enjoy them for what they are instead of focusing on the future outcome.
3. Do you accept the sense of organization that others have? Not everything can be organized the way you think is right.

VIRGO

YOUR OWN NATURE WILL TAKE CARE OF ADJUSTING EVERY DETAIL.

Suggestions for the month of Virgo

- The capability to deal with technical procedures which require a wide knowledge of details is always represented by the energy of Virgo.
- Martial arts teachers, pediatricians, librarians, lab technicians, mechanics and people involved in the process of filing and stocking are related to the energy of Virgo.
- Clean, tidy places are the perfect environment for Virgo. Museums, art galleries and libraries are good examples of Virgo energy in our society.

Notes for reflection

1. Do you know what areas of your body are sensitive? Do you know if you could be prone to any ailment or chronic pain?
2. To experience an illness is related with the need to readjust emotionally and mentally.
3. Pettiness prevents us from achieving great goals.

LIBRA

WHEN YOU FIND YOUR SOUL MATE YOU WILL BE BALANCED.

Suggestions for the month of Libra

- The graphic representation of this birth sign is the scale. Libra is naturally searching for balance.
- People from Libra are attracted to professions related to art and aesthetics. Diplomatic occupations and public relations are also associated with this birth sign as they also look for balance and harmony in other levels of human experience.
- Harmonic landscapes, with lakes and hills and a gentle temperature, are representative of Libra.

Notes for reflection

1. Libra develops in the area of relations. Do you accept the other?
2. A scale cannot be balanced if we put all the weight on one side. Do you balance your scale?
3. Accept the positive and negative sides of your life. This way you can find harmony.

SCORPIO

WHEN YOU LET GO AND SURRENDER, YOU WILL TRANSFORM.

Suggestions for the month of Scorpio
- Scorpio feels like energy of emotional transformation.
- People from Scorpio can be involved with careers where deep study of a subject takes place. Psychiatrists, surgeons and geologists are examples of this tendency. Scuba divers and miners carry out tasks that associate with Scorpio's energy.
- Dark mountains and caves can represent the landscape we identify with Scorpio. Exuberant forests at night also keep a strong relation with the energy of this birth sign.

Notes for reflection
1. Like a tree, the path to transformation starts from the deepest roots and grows to reach the sky.
2. Can you adapt to the circumstances when you face a crisis?
3. Do you control the circumstances? Are the circumstances controlling you?

SAGITTARIUS

FIND YOUR REAL TARGET BEFORE SHOOTING THE ARROW.

Suggestions for the month of Sagittarius
- The search for expansion and truth is related to Sagittarius.
- Sagittarius relates well to traveling. Philosophy also holds a strong relation with the energy of this birth sign.
- Professionals like pilots, air hostesses, priests, judges and teachers are using the energy of Sagittarius.
- Open spaces where expansion and light are predominant belong to the energy of Sagittarius.

Notes for reflection
1. In the search for truth, judgment can become a dangerous friend.
2. Do you exaggerate your faith in yourself? Clarify who you are before expanding.
3. Do you tolerate and respect the truth from others?

CAPRICORN

LET STRUCTURES HOLD YOUR FOUNDATION, BUT NOT LIMIT YOUR GROWTH.

Suggestions for the month of Capricorn

- The energy of Capricorn is related to cycles and regular laws that help members of a group to cohabit.
- Climbers, hermits, inventors and researchers can be associated with the energy of Capricorn.
- High mountains and in general great heights with rocky hills are the landscape of Capricorn.

Notes for reflection

1. Do you have difficulty to kneel? Internal flexibility and adaptability is reflected in our bodies' flexibility.
2. How well do your goals satisfy you?
3. Is it taking you you too long to reach your goal?

AQUARIUS

WHEN YOU KNOW YOURSELF AND DETACH FROM OLD STRUCTURES, YOU FIND FREEDOM.

Suggestions for the month of Aquarius

- The energy of Aquarius needs to destroy old structures to renew social groups with new ideas.
- Aquarius is an Air sign and people involved with the skies, either by flying airplanes, sky diving, UFO observation or science fiction are using the energy of this birth sign.
- Electricity is also associated with the energy of Aquarius.
- The ideal environment for Aquarius is close to the sky. Either looking at the stars in an observatory or flying an airplane.

Notes for reflection

1. How do you feel when you face sudden change? Analyze whether sudden changes impose great effort on you or if you adapt easily and can overcome these quickly.
2. How do you feel in a group? Do you need to let others know that you are different? In Aquarius we want to show that we are different and special and this energy can be shown creatively or aggressively.
3. In which aspect of your life do you feel that you are original? To be different speaks of our capability to create something special that can help our group.

PISCES

IF YOU ARE ABLE TO FEEL YOUR HEART, YOU CAN FEEL THE HEART OF THE UNIVERSE.

Suggestions for the month of Pisces

- The energy of Pisces speaks about a supreme sensitivity. People who can feel it are immersed like a fish in the ocean, perceiving all vibrations close and distant.
- There is a story about a man who was allowed to visit Heaven and Hell. When he arrived in Hell, he saw a great dinner table full of exquisite meals. However, the people sitting at the table suffered terribly as they held long cutlery they could not put in their mouths. Then this man went to Heaven and was surprised to see the same table and long cutlery. The difference was that each person was feeding the person sitting across the table and all of them had the chance to taste the delicious food that had been placed in front of them.
- Classic dancers, musicians, swimming instructors, sailors, scuba divers and health workers in hospitals are using the energy of Pisces. Activities related with deep sensitivity, with music or with mysticism, belong to Pisces.
- Oceans and the sea-side are typical environments of Pisces. Quiet places and areas for meditation have the energy of this birth sign.

Notes for reflection

1. Do you always sacrifice and suffer? Have you ever asked yourself what is the reason for this suffering? You might be taking responsibility over matters that do not belong to you. To help others does not mean to sacrifice our own necessities.
2. Always take good care of your feet. Massage them often and give yourself the pleasure of walking barefoot as much as you can.
3. Do you know where your feelings end and the other's feelings begin?
4. The universe is harmonious and when we are in the right place at the right time, it will lead us towards our destiny without pain or suffering.